Pure Guidance

Written by:
Master Rashid

Cadmus Publishing
www.cadmuspublishing.com

Acknowledgments

I first have to acknowledge my creator for without him nothing is possible. Be his helper. All things are!

Next, I have to thank my mother. A strong woman that did for me when she carried a heavy load, as well. To my sister, Lady who became a breath of fresh air. To my sister, Margaret. It is you that showed me what perfection can be. To my brothers George and Alfred. It was my missing y'all that took me places. To my brothers Ronald and Kenneth, I know I'm trying to better myself so I can measure up. To Ronald and Hasan I love you and want you to be able to count on me. Khalid, Hakiem, Devin, and George know I love you unconditionally. To Big Hak, Lil Bro I love you and will protect you always. Lil Hak, I miss you and love you. Sorry I wasn't there. Latisha and Ajeenah, I love you beyond the sky. Raniya "Baby" I love you! Monique, you are my heart. I love you, know that. Khadijah, I have a million hugs and a thousand kisses for you. Lil Karriem I love you, Mr. Smooth. Shakeem I love you, Smart guy. Lil Kenneth, I love you unconditionally. Lil Margaret, I love and miss you. Ms. Kayla, I love you. Ms. Aaliyah, I love you. Mr. Kasim, I love you. Kinesha and Taqaisha know that I love you two more than anything in the world. Lastly, KB, I love ya bro, get ya book finished.

This book is dedicated to everyone that finds it hard to rest because they know that they could, should, and can make more of their life. This book is only to help turn your wheels. To ponder something greater. This book is dedicated to prisoners of war (POWs) who are at war with you and battle harder with themselves. If *Pure Guidance* makes sense to you, pass it on so chains and shackles can be removed and the (POWs) can succeed in turning the wheels of their mind.

Lastly, this book is dedicated to those that believe in the creator of all things. Help me, as I seek only to offer *Pure Guidance* to our path. About the Author

Master Rashid was born in Harlem, New York. It was in Harlem that life was a struggle for his family, but love was forever present.

In later years the family would move to the Bronx, White Plains section. It was here Master Rashid who would be educated for a time until he was bitten like so many by the serpent (Devil). It was not until the prison of a cage found Master Rashid. That he saw the bigger picture. Master Rashid found himself hungry for knowledge with nothing but time and money to his studies as he became free. Freedom he never felt before. Freedom he wanted to share with the hope that if he could only help one. Then it would be only one. That one would help two and the healing would be done. Anything can be made possible with the creator on your side. Master Rashid only hopes to be an aid to those that will take his hand and the handhold will form a chain of many men, women, and children. So, that knowledge is exchanged and hearts are softened. For the promise of our creator is grand. We must help each other as we come from one father and one mother. Bless be all that stand upon the truth.

Today, be good to yourself!
"Know that you are loved."
(Self-worth)

You have a voice, use it!
"Gather your thoughts, speak."
(Courage)

Never fail yourself!
"You must trust you."
(Belief)

Control your thoughts!
"Be not a slave to your emotions."
(Mastery)

Listen more, speak less!
"It's listening that helps pass a test."
(Attentive)

Life can be short!
"So live your best with your time."
(Appreciate)

We didn't pick our family!
"Though we can measure and pick our friends."
(Audit)

Why pick a fight with someone else!
"You seem to be in a no-end battle with yourself."
(Awaken)

There isn't a closed door!
"Look at it as if the door has not opened yet."
(Perception)

Close your eyes, see a better place!
"With eyes wide open, make it to that better place."
(Act)

If calling friends/family fails!
"Bow in prayer. He answers everything."
(Surrender)

Money isn't the solution to your problem!
"Money is the quick fix and the serpent's slippery
slide."
(Peril)

If you give today!
"Your tomorrow will be blessed."
(Share)

Master yourself first!
"Be helpful to others later."
(Prepare)

Teach them to pray!
"As prayer is the gift that keeps giving."
(Lead)

If shooting for the stars is too big!
"Then open your mind a bit more."
(Will)

Change the way you think!
"Big things will come your way."
(Shift)

What you cling to inside yourself!
"You manifest in your words and deeds."
(Reflect)

You can't outrun yourself!
"But you can stop tripping yourself up."
(Focus)

It can't hurt to be a better you!
"You can make it fatal by not trying."
(Embody)

Have you forgiveness!
"Lest ye be one seeking forgiveness."
(Release)

Live life on life's terms!
"For the instructions are easy. The terms, already written."
(Understanding)

Keep your circle small!
"You spend less time watching for snakes."
(Limit)

Keep an open mind and a caring heart!
"See you the blessing shower in."
(Mindful)

If you rose from your bed today!
"Fall in prayer because we know not if tomorrow
shall come."
(Love)

We all look for something!
"Though what we need is right in plain sight."
(Knowledge)

You don't need money to be rich!
"Learn to be rich in family, friends and an uncorrupt-
ed soul."
(Value)

If you look for the puzzle!
"The game you seek shall be found. "Keep your fo-
cus on your path!
"Make your path your focus."
(Train)

Don't be so quick to give up!
"Learn more so to give in."
(Humility)

You are worried about them!
"Though it is you on the ledge alone."
(Introversion)

You feed your face all day!
"Though starve your soul of food."
(Scrutiny)

You seek to be free!
"Though you cage your mind."
(Search)

Before you say something foolish!
"Think of the words before you use them."
(Salutary)

Stand firm on the statement made!
"Obtain knowledge lest ye make yourself the fool."
(Propagate)

It is better to stand alone with purpose!
"Then to fall in a circle of clowns."
(Scruples)

Make each step count for something!
"For ye shall find your heading nowhere fast."
(Prosaic)

You seek an easy answer!
"Though you refuse to do the easier work to find it."
(Rectify)

Have a thirst for knowledge!
"Drink from the well that shall never dry."
(Conscience)

If you dig deep in yourself!
"You may surprise yourself as to what you pull out."
(Refinement)

If you can't live for today!
"Then you shall live for your tomorrows."
(Amend)

Life isn't hard at all!
"Though the way we choose to live it isn't easy."
(Intercept)

You can be the first or last in the race!
"The finish line is the same distance for both win-
ners."
(Integrity)

If you keep your eyes in the sky!
"You miss the blessings going by."
(Contemplate)

If you have a flame in your heart!
"Your conviction is heard in your voice and seen in
your walk."
(Consistency)

You don't have to follow the flow!
"Dare to set the trend."
(Demonstrate)

You have a mind of your own!
"Don't be scared to use it."
(Enterprise)

Just because it looks good!
"It doesn't mean it is for you."
(Avoidance)

Keep it close to the vest!
"You keep low worries and stress."
(Envelopes)

Don't worry about the voices in the crowd!
"More important are the voices that don't speak out
loud."
(Anticipate)

You can plan for success!
"But following a successful plan is better."
(Achievements)

You can pretend to be wise!
"But know you can't fool anyone but a fool."
(Deterrent)

You can make an effort and be forgiven!
"Though waiting too long, apologies may be reject-
ed."
(Repentance)

They may love to hate you!
"Though know they hate themselves worse."
(Evident)

It might seem so easy!
"But it's a struggle to hold on to something worth
keeping."
(Fortify)

You have strengthen your body!
"Doesn't your soul deserve the same empowerment?"
(Enrichment)

If your brain could keep up with your mouth!
"You would be rich with a thousand words coming
out."
(Despise)

Seek to enjoy life's riches!
"Find your path, stick to it."
(Persevere)

You wash the dirt off your hands!
"But your soul reeks of your dirty deed."
(Remorseful)

If you don't believe in yourself!
"Can you blame them if they don't believe in you
either?"
(Dignity)

Don't put your emotions on display!
"If you can't handle the prying and the play."
(Endurance)

Life isn't always going to seem grand!
"But life is worth living so plan and then plan."
(Endeavor)

You can try to do something!
"But the better course is to just do a thing."
(Ignition)

Today let your vision take flight!
"Tomorrow soar to heights unknown."
(Cultivation)

Make that step you take count!
"It's better to step somewhere than to step nowhere."
(Appropriation)

Just for today love without a filter!
"Just for today, put others before yourself."
(Sacrifice)

Why ask when you know!
"Change it, you do better and get better."
(Rotation)

If you feel shame in your deed!
"Maybe prayer should be offered on bended knees."
(Atonement)

Around every corner is a fresh start!
"Dare yourself to be bold."
(Attainment)

Life may be full of hurdles!
"After you clear the first one the next seems easier."
(Critic)

Do more today!
"Tomorrow you see results."
(Provident)

If you want a great future!
"Live in the now though plan your tomorrow out."
(Strategist)

Don't worry what they think!
"Worry when you are no longer their topic."
(Phobias)

Don't try to fit in!
"It's better to stand out."
(Significant)

You seek positive resolution!
"Enter your inner self ye find the key to unlock the
solution."
(Requisite)

Don't dwell too long on the past!
"The present is now and your future will pass you
by."
(Alleviate)

Deal with what you can!
"Don't dwell on what could be, make happen what
need to be."
(Procure)

If you can't trust yourself!
"Something must change in that person."
(Repudiate)

Stop, take a breath!
"You aren't a machine."
(Relaxation)

You believe it!
"Then you make it be."
(Ingenious)

Your mind is your greatest weapon!
"Keep your arsenal stocked with knowledge."
(Proficiency)

You are changing and growing!
"The fruits of your labor are showing."
(Prosperity)

Get up, make it happen today!
"Tomorrow isn't promised and the future is far away."
(Cumulative)

You have to push yourself!
"If not ye then who else shall."
(Motivation)

You have your eyes open!
"But blind still as your mind is shut."
(Partition)

All it takes is one!
"You have it in you to be that one."
(Paragon)

One man can move a mountain!
"You just need the proper plan and tools."
(Manifestation)

Speak your truth!
"You deserve to be heard."
(Clarification)

Be the voice of empowerment!
"Embody the flame of the struggle, share the fire of
the movement."
(Deliverance)

The healing shall begin!
"When you step back and look within."
(Reflection)

Just because you think it doesn't make it so!
"Just because you think it, no one needs to know."
(Consequences)

Live in life with a purpose!
"Make this life as purposeful as you can."
(Peruse)

Don't give up on living life!
"Because life won't give up on you."
(Clairvoyance)

You don't have to lie to kick it!
"The truth sounds better any day."
(Honesty)

You need to look in the mirror!
"Ask how you can help or get out of their way."
(Hindrance)

You are in a struggle with yourself!
"Step to the side, get out your way."
(Suffocation)

The world is full of cats and dogs!
"So, why are you chasing your tail?"
(Excel)

This earth is your candy shop!
"Search it out and find your dreams delight."
(Embark)

Look in your heart!
"Then find your path."
(Essential)

You have viewed life with a narrow scope!
"Shift your thoughts and enlarge your vision for bigger and better things."
(Commence)

Don't do a good deed for recognition alone!
"Do the deed, for you're sharing a part of your soul."
(Embrace)

You are never truly alone!
"You have a friend closer to you than yourself."
(Consciousness)

Today was once tomorrow and tomorrow was once yesterday!
"Your future is built on the back of today's tomor-rows and yesterday's plan for success here and now."
(Careerism)

Don't sit waiting for love!
"Love is sitting waiting for you."
(Arriviste)

Live love be in life!
"All else shall fall in place."
(Boon)

Don't make excuses, they all do!
"Live up to your potential, you deserve the reward."
(Boost)

A child is a blessing to life!
"Be thankful for such a blessing."
(Reverence)

Only knowledge keeps you safe!
"So study plan and study some more danger lurks
behind many corners and a lot of doors." (Avarice)

Too much of anything can cause you pain!
"Some pains even time won't heal away."
(Gingerly)

Why cry, why pry on a soul you'll let die!
"If you cry then you must try when you pry to rekin-
dle the flame of the soul before it goes bye." (Perti-
nent)

Freedom comes with a price; some will sell their soul
in the name of liberty!
"Though chained and shackled is their mind."
(Intricate)

Only they firmly grounded in belief!
"Cannot and will not be moved from the path of
truth."
(Introvert)

What will you give of yourself!
"Your reward will come back tenfold."
(Devotion)

Today I think of someone else!
"Tomorrow you may be the one being thought of."
(Charitable)

If you think you can grow rich!
"Start thinking today, build your empire tomorrow."
(Embellishment)

The time is now the place is here!
"What you make happen is on you."
(Ascension)

If you seek all your benefits now!
"What have you stored away for later."
(Contemplation)

Go find you a better helper than he!
"What ye find is a troubling task indeed."
(Betrayal)

Call on your friend that never fails!
"Only he can make true your dreams and fairy tales."
(Benefactor)

Keep ye a firm grip!
"Easy is it to lose focus."
(Perceptible)

Many fight back demons!
"While the monster goes unchecked."
(Degenerative)

If you want the best of anything!
"You have to put your all into it."
(Concentrate)

Life can be hard on you or you can be hard on life!
"The path you choose is within you."
(Empirical)

Never give up on your worst fears!
"Don't stop believing in the hope of tomorrow."
(Maximization)

Pick your friends wisely!
"As tomorrow foe was today's friend."
(Capricious)

Live life as each day is your last!
"As we know not if tomorrow will come."
(Deviation)

Life can be hard, never give up, believe in the path
you're on!
"For the hope of tomorrow is just a hilltop away."
(Benediction)

Your opinion isn't alone!
"Mill it around before you set final judgment."
(Consultant)

You ran all you had out the door!
"Alone you now sit forevermore."
(Accountability)

Be the beacon of light!
"Receive the best reward."
(Charismatic)

You focus all your energy on what you don't have!
"As opposed to being thankful for that which you
have."
(Contentment)

You can't control what you don't possess!
"But you can focus your attention on that which you
were blessed."
(Extol)

Throw not blessings out the window!
"They come so far in between."
(Fidelity)

If I had the knowledge of yesterday, today!
"My tomorrow would present plans for my future."
(Acknowledge)

If you find yourself in a dark place!
"Seek help higher than yourself. The light will shine
in."
(Mediation)

Dare to be more than a dreamer!
"Make real what you envision in dreams."
(Inspire)

Let people say what they will!
"You do that which brings you joy."
(Splendor)

Fear isn't a sign of weakness as commonly used!
"Fear is a strength and weapon if controlled."
(Regulation)

Be good to those that you love!
"For tomorrow may come too late."
(Conserve)

Fear not doing the right thing!
"Shame and fear should accompany you when you
don't."
(Proprieties)

Never allow anyone in your heart!
"If tomorrow reservation were made to cut it out."
(Transitory)

Make sure any decision you make!
"Isn't one that you later harbor regrets."
(Repulsive)

If you hate yourself today!
"Then no time like the present to address your is-
sues."
(Neutralize)

Balance out the scales!
"Good morals and high values you'll never fail."
(Scrutinize)

They see a closed door!
"You should see a door that hasn't been opened yet
by you."
(Potential)

Blessed be he that is the giver!
"To the needy."
(Successful)

If you find yourself outnumbered!
"Outwit and outclass to even the odds."
(Preemptive)

Make decisions based on facts!
"Emotions only cloud your judgment."
(Obstruction)

Everyone seeks to wear the crown!
"Though no one wants to bear the weight that comes
with it."
(Perspicacity)

Why fear the laws of the people!
"When the creator of all laws have more merits and
stiffer penalties."
(Relinquish)

Every soul shall be freed from the flesh!
"What deeds have you stored and are waiting upon
your death."
(Notability)

"I fall to you in complete submission. I began my first wake with you. My final sleep is yours to command. Surely your promise has never failed when you find it my time to move on from this place, please let me leave with no regrets and many well-wishers to send me home." Amen

"I call on you my creator for guidance as I am lost on this globe spinning fast my footing unfirm my thoughts a jumbo mix. I humbly beseech your aid for without such I am of the losers." Amen

"How do I cast my glance upon something as small as the ant and not be beyond awe of its creator. I have spent my hours amazed at the structure and communication between the tiny ant. How can I not believe you exist beyond time or space. Everywhere but nowhere having no beginning with no end. I start my day with praise to your glory." Amen

"When I found myself in fear you held me close letting me know I wasn't alone. You sheltered me when I had no home. You filled my stomach when it was touching upon my back. It was continuous blessings given without any request made in between how can I possibly deny you love me." Amen

"How can it ever be said that you aren't the author of this grand design? Yet none still understand the wonders of the mind, none has created space or time corrections are made in all said finds. Yet foolishly they deny that you are the author of this grand design until they need you calling out your name. Then they know how to praise them, giving you all the glory as you rightly deserve. Now understanding there is one bigger than themselves."

"I have walked upon your earth uncertain of away until you became my guide. It was you that gave me spring in my step. When I felt that I couldn't go on and ran upon fumes. It was you that carried me upon my path. I have never needed as you have always provided for me. I never wake or sleep without marveling upon your greatness."

"I watched lost in thought as the sun slowly fell from the sky. I wonder how the pinkish-red can evenly blanket the once blue sky. Birds seem to know to say good night as they soar on by as the sun seems to kiss the sea. For the night I can only sit and wonder my thoughts upon your high greatness marveling all Marvel talents beyond raw. Mere mortals' words shall never express or contain powers above any reachable plains. I can only fall humbly upon bended knee seeking to be enlightened, released from the pressure holding me in bondage from being my true self."

"Just for a moment clear my head of the clutter. Just for a second allow me to breathe a fresh breath. Just for an hour relieve me of pains just for the day allow me to love you the right way. It is only you that has this power and control. I came to you just because I know."

Just because you can!
"Don't mean you should."
(Section)

They aren't trying to be you!
"So, why are you trying to be like them?"
(Degrade)

If you only think negatively!
"Any wonder you get what you got."
(Pessimistic)

You worry then pray, you pray then complain!
"Why pray if you still do both."
(Nonsensical)

"In life, second chances don't come often so if you are one of the lucky ones use your next chances wisely as there may be no more."
(Consideration)

If only for one day!
"Take time out for yourself, know your limits."
(Consecrate)

"I've stood upon some of the highest peaks swore the wind called me but it can't speak. I've found myself climbing high in some of the highest trees. I swore I saw a bird's eye wink as she flew by me but surely this can't be. I've even found myself swimming in the deepest blue sea swore I saw fish wave a fin and blow a kiss at me. I know this can't be what's happen to me, maybe just maybe these signs are the highest communicating with me, for marvels for him is easy to make be." The crown doesn't come easy, it's a lot of work to be king!

"So seek the crown of your craft."

(Affirmation)

Treat your woman like the queen!
"In her heart, you'll be her king."
(Affectionate)

"Sacrifices were made to get you there. What are you willing to sacrifice to get you where you need to be?" (Schematic)

Don't ruin a good thing behind a rumor!
"Obtain your facts. Then still don't be quick to act."
(Rationality)

Don't be your saboteur!
"Many sabotage their success yet fail to understand
they are the author of the wrongdoing."
(Comprehend)

Don't be the deer stuck in the headlights!
"As you may find that you were struck harder than
the deer."
(Precaution)

You were cast from the most beautiful mold!
"Though how easy and cheaply you'll sell your soul."
(Ravage)

Keep it moving on your course!
"A pause in movement will get you lost."
(Focus)

All you do is make it done in his name!
"Your call shall be answered and your work shall not
be in vain."
(Faithful)

Judge not by one's outer shell!
"That which the heart possesses cannot be com-
pared."
(Quintessence)

Don't other's opinions matter!
"Yes, but have more faith in your brain."
(Propitious)

Give less to your desire of lust!
"Focus heavily on what you need."
(Inviolable)

Why look for the magic!
"When you can make magic."
(Opportunist)

How can you be found!
"If you have yet to know you're lost."
(Noxious)

Never take more than you need!
"The fire awaits for many driven by greed."
(Obscene)

"I had a dream that I sat upon a cloud. There was a voice instructing me to look down. I swear I saw nothing but beautiful sights. I saw wonderful days, some milled around and the children played. I saw beautiful nights, it seemed like every star was present, the moon shone so brightly. The voice instructed what once was, can surely be again when you awake convey my message friend. So, I've woken up conveying that which I was told hoping that I can reach like-minded souls as I know my lord hasn't touched me alone."More money can equal more sin! "The path you take shall be judged at your end." (Requital)

There are many lost sheep!
"Though the wolf needs to snatch only one."
(Incorrigible)

Why look to him for the answer!
"When he lives his life he doesn't have a clue."
(Indulgence)

If you believe in life tomorrow then believe in death today!
"As we can't see when it's our time to prepare."
(Imaginable)

You should prepare for your problems!
"As opposed to waiting for your problems to come along."
(Logical)

When in the dark you look for the light!
"When you find yourself in a dark place let happy
thoughts light your way."
(Moxie)

Stay true to your friends!
"As you shall find, good ones are rare."
(Precious)

Step up to the plate it could be your home run today!
"Though how will you know if you sit out the whole
game?"
(Initiative)

The measure of a man isn't how hard he beats upon
his chest or muscles flex!
"He is measured by how he thinketh and how he han-
dles his test."
(Gallant)

The life of this world is truly a test!
"You will be judged by your actions for a better life
after this, study hard cause you don't want to be
missed."
(Enviable)

I seek thy aid as I have no better protector than you!
"If you turn your back I know not what I'll do."
(Emphasis)

Stay focused on your present!
"Let the future work itself out." Life is very special. A gift!
"Don't live life as if you have a spare."
(Immeasurable)

If you take care of your business!
"Look for your proper preparation to take care of
you."
(Intimate)

Most look to the sky for their pie!
"Instead of baking it themselves."
(Expedition)

Anger is like wildfire!
"If not quickly under control. It'll consume all in its
path."
(Interpolation)

Nothing in life truly belongs to you!
"Just know the true owner can and will come for their
property. Be thankful for your loan."
(Inevitable)

You can let what happens be!
"Though know it may not be as sweet as a dream."
(Discern)

Don't box yourself in!
"You have so much room at hand use it."
(Chronograph)

Just take a breath!
"You need not always rush."
(Calculation)

You are the author of your prison!
"The key to freedom is in the mind."
(Thinker)

You don't have to go through that door!
"Find another way to get where you need to be."
(Magnification)

About the Author

Master Rashid was born in Harlem, New York. It was in Harlem that life was a struggle for his family, but love was forever present.

In later years, the family would move to Bronx, White Plains section. It was here Master Rashid, who would be educated for a time until he was bitten like so many by the serpent (Devil). It was not until the prison of a cage found Master Rashid that he saw the bigger picture. Master Rashid found himself hungry for knowledge with nothing but time and money to his studies as he became free. Freedom he never felt before. Freedom he wanted to share with the hope that, if he could only help one, then it would be only one. That one would help two and the healing would be done. Anything can be made possible with the creator on your side. Master Rashid only hopes to be an aid to those that will take his hand and the handhold will form a chain of many men, women, and children. So that knowledge is exchanged and hearts are softened. For the promise of our creator is grand. We must help each other as we come from one father and one mother. Bless be all that stand upon the truth.

CPSIA information can be obtained
at www.ICGtesting.com
Printed in the USA
BVHW090833200921
617100BV00007B/94